CO...

ANTIQUE SILVER MARKS

Anna Selby
and
The Diagram Group

HarperCollinsPublishers

This edition specially produced in 1995 for
Orpheus Publications Ltd by arrangement with
HarperCollins *Publishers*
77–85 Fulham Palace Road
Hammersmith, London W6 8JB

A Diagram book first published as Collins Gem
Antique Marks and created by Diagram Visual
Information Limited of 195 Kentish Town Road,
London NW5 8SY

First published 1994

© Diagram Visual Information Limited 1994

ISBN 0 583 31983 1

Printed in Great Britain by
HarperCollins Manufacturing, Glasgow

Contents

Hallmarks on silver, gold and platinum

Silver and gold have long been prized for their useful and attractive properties. Gold was one of the first metals to be discovered. Being soft and easy to work, colourful, bright and resistant to corrosion, it was ideal for jewellery and other decorative objects. Its scarcity ensured that its value remained high. Silver is harder and less scarce than gold, and thus more widely used in everyday life. Both silver and gold have been mined in Britain since Roman times, in modest quantities. Platinum was unknown in Europe until 1600, only became available commercially in the 19th century, and has only been regulated in Britain since 1975. Used mainly for jewellery, it is more precious than gold. The high value of these three metals makes it essential to have legally enforced standards of purity. The craft of the silversmith has been regulated by Parliamentary Acts and Royal Ordinances since the late 12th century. Since 1 January 1975, a simplified scheme of hallmarks has been in use for British silver, gold and platinum, as directed by the Hallmarking Act of 1973.

PRE-1975 HALLMARKS AND WHAT THEY MEAN

Under the British regulations, any object made of silver or gold is stamped with various 'hallmarks' which enable us to tell when it was made, by whom, where it was manufactured or tested for purity, and, most important of all, how pure it is. The term 'hallmark' is derived from Goldsmiths' Hall, the guild hall of the London Goldsmiths' Company, the body which oversaw the first assay marks in Britain. In 1300, the Sterling standard was established at 925 parts of silver per 1000 in an object, just as in English coinage. No object was allowed to leave the craftsman's hands until it had been assayed (tested) and marked with a punch depicting a leopard's head, a mark which is still used on London silver. Other assay offices were established in the English provinces, and in Scotland and Ireland, and all but the smallest had their own mark of origin.

From 1363, each craftsman was required to add his own 'maker's mark' and to register it.

From 1478, a 'date mark' was required to be struck, consisting of a letter of the alphabet which signified the year in which the piece had been assayed. This made it possible to trace the 'Keeper of the Touch' who had assayed a particular piece, in case of later disputes as to purity. It now allows us to determine an accurate date for any piece of British plate.

A 'duty mark' depicting the head of the current monarch is found on plate assayed between 1784 and 1890, as proof that a tax on silver goods had been paid by the maker. The duty mark should not be confused with later commemorative stamps which mark special occasions such as Coronations and Jubilees.

Marks of origin on British silver to 1974

The mark of origin, or assay office mark, identifies the town or city where the item in question was assayed, and probably manufactured. Since 1300, London has used the leopard's head (**1**) (sometimes crowned, sometimes not). An exception is the period 1697–1720 when the 'lion's head erased' (**2**) was used, when the Britannia standard replaced the Sterling standard for English silver. At Edinburgh, the earliest Scottish assay office, the mark of origin has always been a three-towered castle (**3**). Dublin has used a harp crowned (**4**) since the mid 17th century. As further examples, Birmingham has long used an anchor (**5**), and Sheffield used a crown (**6**) for many years. More specific information on marks of origin will be found in the introductions to the tables of each city's hallmarks, later in the present chapter.

Sample marks of origin

| 1 | 2 | 3 | 4 | 5 | 6 |

Makers' marks

Since 1363, silversmiths have been required to stamp their work with a registered mark. Thus one can identify the maker of a particular piece – at least if it was made after about 1666, when the earlier registers at Goldsmiths' Hall were burnt in the Great Fire of London. At first the custom was to use a rebus (for example a picture of a fox for a silversmith whose surname was Fox) and initials combined in one mark. From 1697, makers were required by law to use the first two letters of their surnames (**a, b**), but from 1720 initials again became the norm (**c, d**), sometimes with a symbol added (**e, f**).

In Scotland before about 1700, makers commonly used a monogram (**g, h**), but this died out to be replaced by plain initials (**i**). Some used their full surname (**j**). In the case of factories or firms (**k**), the maker's mark is often called the 'sponsor's mark'.

Sample makers' marks

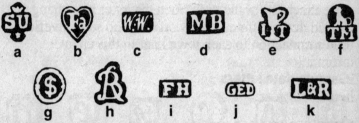

a Thomas Sutton, London 1711
b John Farnell, London 1714
c William Woodward, London 1741
d Mathew Boulton, Birmingham 1790
e John Tuite, London 1739
f Thomas Morse, London 1720
g James Sympsone, Edinburgh 1687
h Robert Brook, Glasgow 1673
i Francis Howden, Edinburgh 1781
j Dougal Ged, Edinburgh 1734
k Lothian and Robertson, Edinburgh 1746

Date letters to 1974
Date letters were introduced in England from 1478, in Scotland (Edinburgh) from 1681, and in Ireland (Dublin) from 1638. The date letter system means that every item of hallmarked silver (and gold) carries a stamp indicating the year when it was assayed. The date stamp takes the form of a letter of the alphabet,

changed to the next letter annually in a regular cycle, rather like present-day car registrations. Different assay offices have used different cycles, omitting various letters of the alphabet to form sequences lasting from 19 to 26 years. 'I' was often used for 'J'. Each new cycle was given a new style of lettering and shape of shield, so as to distinguish one cycle from another. The exact day of the year when the letter was changed varied at the different assay offices, and so is given in the introduction to each town later in this chapter.

Sample date letters

| 1 | 2 | 3 | 4 | 5 | 6 |

1 London 1561   4 Chester 1742
2 London 1936   5 Dublin 1662
3 Birmingham 1891 6 Edinburgh 1968

Standard marks to 1974
In England before 1544, the Sterling silver standard of 92.5% purity (925 parts per 1000) was vouched for by the leopard's head mark of the London Assay Office (a). In 1544, Henry VIII debased the coinage to only one third silver, and so a specific 'standard mark' showing a lion passant (b) was introduced, to be marked on items which met the Sterling standard. In 1697, the Sterling standard was replaced by the Britannia standard of 95.84% purity (958.4 parts per 1000), to stop the melting down of coins for plate. The Britannia figure (c) now replaced the lion passant as the

standard mark, and the lion's head erased (**d**) replaced the leopard's head as the mark of origin. From 1720, the Sterling standard and its lion passant mark were reintroduced, but silver of the higher standard (although less common) continued to be marked with Britannia and the lion's head erased right up to 1974. Edinburgh and Glasgow used different standards of fineness (as described on page 36) until 1836, when they adopted the Sterling and Britannia standards.

Sample standard marks

a   b   c   d

Duty marks 1784–1890

Between 1784 and 1890 a duty (tax) was imposed on silver in Britain. To prove that the duty had been paid by the silversmith, an extra mark depicting the head of the current king or queen was struck on most items of silverware produced in England in those years. (In Dublin the duty was imposed only from 1807 and in Glasgow from 1819.) Silversmiths had many tricks to avoid paying duty, so the mark is not always present.

Duty marks

1   2   3   4

1 George III (1760–1820)   3 William IV (1830–1837)
2 George IV (1820–1830)   4 Victoria (1837–1901)

Commemorative marks

Special marks have been added in certain calendar years to mark notable occasions. A mark with the heads of both King George V and Queen Mary (**1**) was used to mark their Silver Jubilee in 1935. The Coronation of Elizabeth II in 1953 was commemorated with a mark of the Queen's head (**2**). A similar mark (**3**) was used again to mark her Jubilee in 1977. Special commemorative marks have also been used by the Dublin, Birmingham and Sheffield assay offices to celebrate various anniversaries in the 1970s and 1980s. Because of the exact time of year when the date letter was changed at a particular assay office, such marks may appear not only with the date letter of the year commemorated, but also with that of the year before or the one after.

1   **2**   **3**

Marks on foreign silver to 1974

From 1867, a letter F (**a**) was stamped on foreign plate imported into Britain. From 1904, the decimal value of the Sterling (**b**) and Britannia (**c**) standards was marked on imported silver which met those standards, and each assay office had a special mark of origin, as used on imported gold, but in an oval shield.

a   **b**   **c**

THE HALLMARKING ACT OF 1973

In 1973 a new Act of Parliament was passed for regulating and simplifying the law regarding hallmarks on silver, gold and platinum in Britain, and it came into force on 1 January 1975. The Act governs hallmarks at the four remaining assay offices, in London, Edinburgh, Birmingham and Sheffield (but not Dublin, which since 1921 has been the captial of the independent Irish Republic). All items weighing more than 7.8 grams must be hallmarked before they can be described as silver (for gold it is any item above 1 gram, and for platinum above 0.5 gram). There are four hallmarks in total: the registered maker's or sponsor's mark, the standard mark, the mark of origin (assay office mark), and the date letter.

Sample modern silver hallmarks

1   2   3   4

1 Maker's mark   **2** Standard mark
3 Mark of origin   **4** Date letter

Standard marks from 1975

On Sterling silver, the London, Birmingham and Sheffield Assay Offices still use the traditional lion passant (**a**), while Edinburgh uses the lion rampant (**b**). At all four offices, the Britannia mark (**c**) is used (without the old accompanying lion's head erased) on silver which meets the Britannia standard.

 a   b   c

Marks of Origin from 1975

Only four assay offices remained open in Britain by 1975. London still uses a leopard's head (**1**). Birmingham still uses its anchor (**2**) and Edinburgh its three-towered castle (**3**). However, Sheffield has adopted a York rose (**4**) to replace the crown which it had used for over 200 years, because the crown risked being confused with a similar mark on gold. Dublin is not affected by the Act, and still uses its harp crowned.

1   **2**   **3**   **4**

Date letters from 1975

The date letter now coincides exactly with the calendar year, it being changed on 1 January every year, and the same style is used by all four British assay offices.

Imported foreign silver from 1975

The marking of imported foreign silver has been simplified and standardized under the 1973 Act. The standard mark consists of the millesimal value in an oval shield (see below). The marks of origin used by the four assay offices are similar to those on foreign gold and platinum, but in an oval shield (see below).

925   **958**
Sterling   Britannia

London   Birmingham   Sheffield   Edinburgh

Convention marks

In the past, UK makers had difficulty exporting British silver and gold, because the hallmarks were not legally recognised abroad. Importers faced similar problems. Therefore the European Free Trade Association has produced a convention on the control and marking of precious metals, and the UK has been a signatory since 1976. Under this arrangement, a set of 'convention marks' is commonly recognized. They consist of a common control mark (see below) giving the standard of fineness, the fineness again in numerals, also a mark of origin and a sponsor's (maker's) mark. These marks are struck in place of, or in addition to, the usual British or foreign marks. The system of convention marks means that precious metals assayed in countries which are signatories can be imported and exported between those countries without being re-assayed.

Control marks

750	Gold	18 carat
585	Gold	14 carat
375	Gold	9 carat
925	Silver	Sterling
950	Platinum	

Note that in the UK, any silver below Sterling (925) standard is not approved. Britannia silver and 22 carat gold are not recognized under the convention.

The British Hallmarking Council

A body called the British Hallmarking Council was established under the 1973 Act, and became operative in 1975. The Council coordinates the activities of the four assay offices, without hindering their independence. Its main responsibility is to ensure that adequate assaying facilities are available in the UK, and to see that laws relating to assaying are adhered to.

READING THE HALLMARK CHARTS IN THIS BOOK

Layout of the hallmark charts

The charts on the pages which follow show the hallmarks associated with each of the towns or cities which have had important assay offices, presented in the order in which the assay offices were established. Within each section, all the variations in the design of that city's mark of origin (**b**) and the standard marks (**c** and sometimes **d**) are illustrated, and these are followed by any duty marks or commemorative marks (**e**) and by the date letters (**f**). Unusual marks are fully explained in special feature panels (**a**). Makers' marks are shown separately in lists at the end of each city's section. Note that the hallmark charts apply primarily to silver (as they show the standard marks for silver), but that the same date letters apply equally to British gold.

Here is a sample of a set of marks which you may be looking for (although they may not appear in this order):

b   c   e   f   h

In the charts they would be shown as follows:

> The duty on silver was doubled in 1797, and so for a short time the king's head was stamped twice   — a

b ———

1798 — f

1799 — g

a Text box for unusual markings
b Mark of origin
c Standard mark
d Possible second standard mark
e Duty or commemorative mark
f Date letter mark
g Text showing year
h Maker's mark (see lists of makers' marks following each city's hallmark charts)

HOW TO READ HALLMARKS

When looking at hallmarks, begin by studying the mark of origin, to find out where the piece was assayed. (If no assay office's mark is present, the piece probably comes from London.) Then turn to the relevant city's section in the tables of hallmarks. Now look at the date letter. This is probably the hardest part of the process. Examine the letter to see whether it is a capital or a small letter, check what kind of script it is in, and note the shape of the shield containing it. Compare these features with the letters in the correct city's tables. Only when you find the example in the table which exactly matches your hallmark can you be confident about its date. Once the place and date of origin are established, it is relatively simple to look up the maker's or sponsor's mark and find out the name of the craftsman or company. Other marks will give extra information, such as whether the piece is Sterling or Britannia silver, whether duty was paid on it, and whether it was made in a Coronation or Jubilee year.

LONDON

The Goldsmiths' Company in London was the first in England authorized to assay and mark gold and silver, after the granting of a Royal Charter in 1327. London has been by far the most important British assay office, both in terms of the high quality of workmanship it maintained, and of the amount and variety of silverware passing through it.

London's mark of origin is a leopard's head, crowned from 1478 to 1821 and thereafter uncrowned. The shape of the head and crown have varied over the years, as has the shield surrounding them. From 1697 until 1720 (while the Britannia standard was in force) the leopard's head was replaced by the lion's head erased and the Britannia mark. From 1784 to 1890, the sovereign's head duty mark was in use.

From 1478 to 1974, London traditionally used a 20-letter sequence (A to U omitting J), with the letter being changed in May each year. Since 1975 all British date letter sequences have been standardized, and are changed on 1 January. In the same year platinum was first assayed and marked here.

The London Assay Office is still in operation.

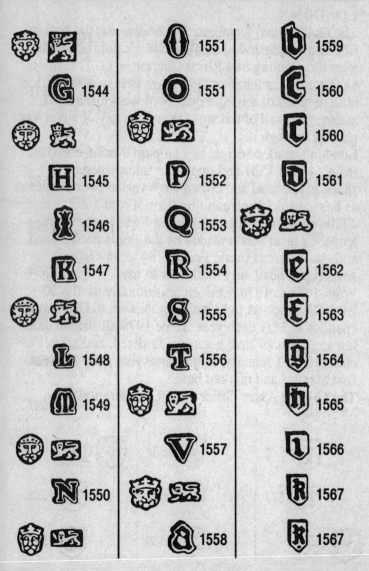

G	1544
H	1545
I	1546
K	1547
L	1548
M	1549
N	1550
O	1551
O	1551
P	1552
Q	1553
R	1554
S	1555
T	1556
V	1557
8	1558
b	1559
C	1560
C	1560
D	1561
e	1562
F	1563
g	1564
h	1565
I	1566
R	1567
k	1567

l	1568	**A**	1578	**N**	1590
m	1569	**B**	1579	**O**	1591
n	1570	**C**	1580	🜲 🦁	
o	1571	**D**	1581	**P**	1592
p	1572	**E**	1582	**Q**	1593
q	1573	**F**	1583	**R**	1594
r	1574	**G**	1584	**S**	1595
s	1575	**H**	1585	**T**	1596
ſ	1575	**I**	1586	**V**	1597
t	1576	**K**	1587	👑 🦁	
u	1577	**L**	1588	**A**	1598
👑 🦁		**M**	1589	**B**	1599

Ⓓ 1600	℗ 1612	f 1623
Ⓓ 1601	Ⓠ 1613	g 1624
Ⓔ 1602	Ⓡ 1614	h 1625
Ⓕ 1603	Ⓢ 1615	i 1626
Ⓖ 1604	Ⓣ 1616	k 1627
ⓗ 1605	Ⓥ 1617	l 1628
Ⓘ 1606	👑 🦁	m 1629
Ⓚ 1607	ⓐ 1618	n 1630
Ⓛ 1608	ⓑ 1619	o 1631
Ⓜ 1609	ⓒ 1620	p 1632
ⓝ 1610	ⓓ 1621	q 1633
Ⓞ 1611	ⓔ 1622	r 1634

🛡 1635	🛡 1646	🛡 1657
🛡 1636	👑 🦁	👑 🦁
🛡 1637	🛡 1647	🛡 1658
👑 🦁	🛡 1648	🛡 1659
🛡 1638	🛡 1649	🛡 1660
🛡 1639	🛡 1650	🛡 1661
🛡 1640	🛡 1651	🛡 1662
🛡 1641	🛡 1652	🛡 1663
🛡 1642	🛡 1653	🛡 1664
🛡 1643	🛡 1654	🛡 1665
🛡 1644	🛡 1655	🛡 1666
🛡 1645	🛡 1656	🛡 1667

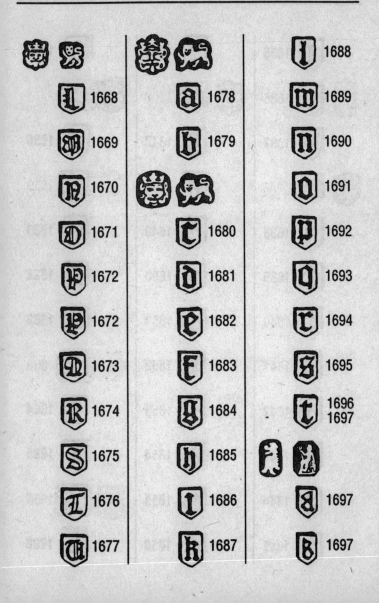

1668
1669
1670
1671
1672
1672
1673
1674
1675
1676
1677

1678
1679
1680
1681
1682
1683
1684
1685
1686
1687

1688
1689
1690
1691
1692
1693
1694
1695
1696
1697
1697
1697

₵ 1698	℞ 1708	D 1719
(lion) (Britannia)	Ф 1709	(leopard head) (lion)
⑤ 1699	⅁ 1710	E 1720
₵ 1700	⑥ 1711	(crown) (lion)
ff 1701	⑥ 1712	F 1721
Ф 1702	⊘ 1713	G 1722
Ф 1702	℧ 1714	H 1723
ℬ 1703	ℭ 1715	(leopard head) (lion)
ℨ 1704	(lion) (Britannia)	I 1724
ℨ 1705	A 1716	K 1725
℮ 1706	B 1717	(leopard head) (lion)
ℊ 1707	C 1718	L 1726

M 1727	**T** 1734	**h** 1743
N 1728	**V** 1735	**i** 1744
		k 1745
From 1716 to 1728, the shield shape for the date letter occasionally varied	**a** 1736	**l** 1746
	b 1737	**m** 1747
	c 1738	**n** 1748
	d 1739	**o** 1749
O 1729	**d** 1739	**p** 1750
P 1730	**e** 1740	**q** 1751
Q 1731	**f** 1741	**r** 1752
R 1732	**g** 1742	**ſ** 1753
S 1733		

𝔱 1754

𝔲 1755

🛡👑 🛡🦁

𝔄 1756

𝔅 1757

ℭ 1758

𝔇 1759

𝔈 1760

𝔉 1761

𝔊 1762

ℌ 1763

𝔍 1764

𝔨 1765

𝔏 1766

𝔐 1767

𝔑 1768

𝔇 1769

𝔓 1770

𝔔 1771

𝔕 1772

𝔖 1773

𝔗 1774

ℭ 1774

𝔘 1775

🛡👑 🛡🦁

Two shield shapes for standard mark found, 1776-1795

From 1776 to 1875, a shield without a point was used for some small articles

𝔞 1776

𝔟 1777

𝔠 1778

𝔡 1779

ⓔ 1780	
f 1781	
g 1782	
h 1783	
i 1784	
k 1785	
l 1786	
m 1787	
n 1788	
o 1789	
p 1790	
q 1791	

r 1792	
s 1793	
t 1794	
u 1795	
A 1796	
B 1797	
C 1798	
D 1799	
E 1800	
F 1801	
G 1802	

H 1803	
I 1804	
K 1805	
L 1806	
M 1807	
N 1808	
O 1809	
P 1810	
Q 1811	
R 1812	
S 1813	
T 1814	

U	1815	k	1825	A	1836
(lion)		l	1826	B	1837
a	1816	m	1827	C	1838
b	1817	n	1828	D	1839
c	1818	o	1829	E	1840
d	1819	p	1830	F	1841
e	1820	q	1831	G	1842
f	1821	r	1832	H	1843
(lion)		s	1833	J	1844
g	1822	t	1834	K	1845
h	1823	u	1835	L	1846
i	1824	(lion)		M	1847

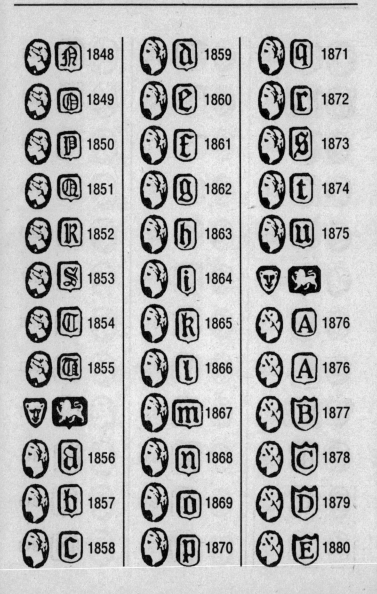

1848	1859	1871
1849	1860	1872
1850	1861	1873
1851	1862	1874
1852	1863	1875
1853	1864	
1854	1865	1876
1855	1866	1876
	1867	1877
1856	1868	1878
1857	1869	1879
1858	1870	1880

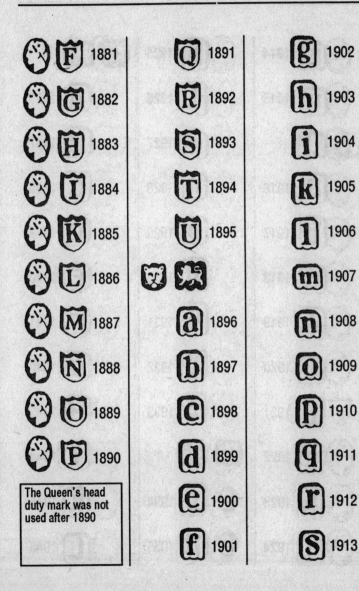

F 1881
G 1882
H 1883
I 1884
K 1885
L 1886
M 1887
N 1888
O 1889
P 1890

The Queen's head duty mark was not used after 1890

Q 1891
R 1892
S 1893
T 1894
U 1895

a 1896
b 1897
c 1898
d 1899
e 1900
f 1901

g 1902
h 1903
i 1904
k 1905
l 1906
m 1907
n 1908
o 1909
p 1910
q 1911
r 1912
s 1913

𝖙 1914	𝖐 1925	🦁 🦁
𝖚 1915	𝖑 1926	A 1936
🦁 🦁	𝖒 1927	B 1937
𝖆 1916	𝖓 1928	C 1938
𝖇 1917	𝖔 1929	D 1939
𝖈 1918	𝖕 1930	E 1940
𝖉 1919	𝖖 1931	F 1941
𝖊 1920	𝖗 1932	G 1942
𝖋 1921	𝖘 1933	H 1943
𝖌 1922	🦁 🦁	I 1944
𝖍 1923	🦁 𝖙 1934	K 1945
𝖎 1924	🦁 𝖚 1935	L 1946

M	1947	a	1956	n	1968
N	1948	b	1957	o	1969
O	1949	c	1958	p	1970
P	1950	d	1959	q	1971
Q	1951	e	1960	r	1972
		f	1961	s	1973
R	1952	g	1962	t	1974
S	1953	h	1963		
		i	1964		
T	1954	k	1965		
U	1955	l	1966		
		m	1967	A	1975

New letter sequence commenced on 1 January 1975, in accordance with the Hallmarking Act passed in 1973

B 1976

C 1977

D 1978

E 1979

F 1980

G 1981

H 1982

J 1983

K 1984

L 1985

M 1986

N 1987

O 1988

P 1989

Q 1990

R 1991

S 1992

T 1993

U 1994

LONDON MAKERS' MARKS

ABS	Adey B Savory		**EC**	Ebenezer Coker
AF	Andrew Fogelberg		**EF**	Edward Feline
SG	& Stephen Gilbert		**ET**	Elizabeth Tuite
AS	Thomas Ash		**EW**	Edward Wigan
BC	Benjamin Cooper		**EY**	Edward Yorke
BS	Benjamin Smith		**FC**	Francis Crump
BS	Benjamin Smith &		**FO**	Thomas Folkingham
BS	Son		**GA**	George Adams
Bu/BU	Thomas Burridge		**GS**	George Smith
CF	Charles Fox or Crispin Fuller		**GS** **WF**	George Smith & William Fearn
CK	Charles F Kandler (star below)		**GW**	George Wintle
CO	Augustin Courtauld (fleur-de-lys above)		**HA**	Pierre Harache (crown above)
CR	Charles Rawlins		**HB**	Hester Bateman
CR **DR**	Christian & David Reid		**HC**	Henry Chawner
CR **GS**	Charles Reilly & George Storer		**HC** **IE**	Henry Chawner & John Emes
CR **WS**	Charles Rawlins & William Summers		**HN**	Hannah Northcote
DH	David Hennell		**IB**	James Bult
DM	Dorothy Mills		**IC**	John Carter
DPW	Dobson, Prior & Williams		**IG**	John Gould
			IH	John Hyatt
DS **BS**	Digby Scott & Benjamin Smith		**IL** **HL**	John & Henry Lias
DS **RS**	Daniel Smith & Robert Sharp		**IL** **HL** **CL**	John, Henry & Charles Lias
			IP	John Pollock

LONDON MAKERS' MARKS (continued)

IS	John Swift or John Scholfield	**PL**	Pierre Platel
IW **IT**	John Walcelon & John Taylor	**PL**	Paul de Lamerie (crown and star above, fleur-de-lys below)
JA	Joseph Angell		
JA **JA**	J & J Aldous	**PS**	Paul Storr
JC	John Cafe	**Py**	Benjamin Pyne (rose and crown above)
JE	John Emes		
JL	John Lias	**RC**	Richard Crossley
LA	Paul de Lamerie (crown and star above)	**RC** **GS**	Richard Crossley & George Smith
LO	Nathaniel Lock	**R** **DH** **H**	Robert & David Hennell
LP	Lewis Pantin		
MC	Mary Chawner	**RE** **EB**	Rebecca Emes & Edward Barnard
ME	Louis Mettayer		
MP	Mary Pantin	**RE** **WE**	Rebecca & William Emes
MS	Mary Sumner	**RG**	Robert Garrard
MS **ES**	Mary & Elizabeth Sumner	**RH**	Robert Hennell
Ne	Anthony Nelme	**RH** **DH**	Robert & David Hennell
NS	Nicholas Sprimont	**RH** **DH** **SH**	Robert, David & Samuel Hennell
PB **AB**	Peter & Anne Bateman		
PB **AB** **WB**	Peter, Anne & William Bateman	**RH** **SH**	Robert & Samuel Hennell
PB **IB**	Peter & Jonathan Bateman	**RM** **RC**	Robert Makepeace & Richard Carter

RM **TM**	Robert & Thomas Makepeace	**TR**	Thomas Robins
Ro	Philip Rolles	**T** **WC** **C**	Thomas & William Chawner
RR	Richard Rugg or Robert Rutland	**WB**	William Burwash
RS	Robert Swanson	**WC**	William Cafe
SA	Stephen Adams	**WE**	William Eaton or William Eley
Sc	William Scarlett		
SC **IC**	S & J Crespell	**WE** **CE** **HE**	William, Charles & Henry Eley
SG	Samuel Godbehere		
SG **EW**	Samuel Godbehere & Edward Wigan	**WE** **GP**	William Eley & George Pierrepont
SL	Gabriel Sleath	**WE** **WF**	William Eley & William Fearn
SM	Samuel Meriton	**WF**	William Fearn
Sp	Thomas Spackman	**WF** **PS**	William Frisbee & Paul Storr
S **WI** **A**	Stephen Adams & William Jury	**WG**	William Grundy
TH	Thomas Heming	**WI**	David Willaume
TH **IC**	Thomas Hannam & John Crouch	**WP**	William Peaston or William Plummer
T & W	Turner & Williams	**WRS**	W R Smiley
TN	Thomas Northcote	**WS**	William Sumner or William Smiley
TO	Thomas Oliphant		
TP **ER**	Thomas Phipps & Edward Robinson	**WT**	William Tweedie
TP **ER** **JP**	Thomas Phipps, Edward Robinson & James Phipps	**W** **WP** **S**	William Shaw & William Priest
TP **IP**	Thomas & James Phipps		

EDINBURGH

Silver was assayed in Edinburgh from the middle of the
15th century, although the first known specimens date
from a century later than that. There was an
Incorporation of Goldsmiths here from at least the
1490s. Over the years Edinburgh has been known
particularly for ecclesiastical and domestic silverware.
The Edinburgh mark of origin is a three-towered castle.
Before 1681 the standard mark took the form of the
Deacon's mark, a monogram of the initials of the
current holder of that office. From 1681 the Deacon's
mark was replaced by the Assay Master's mark, again
consisting of the office-holder's initials. This was
replaced in 1759 by a thistle, which changed in 1975 to
a lion rampant. From 1784 to 1890 the sovereign's head
duty mark was in use.

From 1457 to 1836, Edinburgh used a standard of 916.6
parts of silver per thousand, except in 1489–1555 when
the Standard of Bruges was used (varying from 917 to
946 parts per thousand according to the size of the
object). Only from 1836 was the Sterling standard
adopted at Edinburgh.

Date letters came into use in 1681. Edinburgh generally
used a 25-letter sequence, omitting J (although it was
included in 1789 and 1815). The letter was changed in
October. From 1 January 1975 the standard British date
letter sequence has been used.

The Edinburgh Assay Office is still in operation.
Platinum was first marked here in 1982.

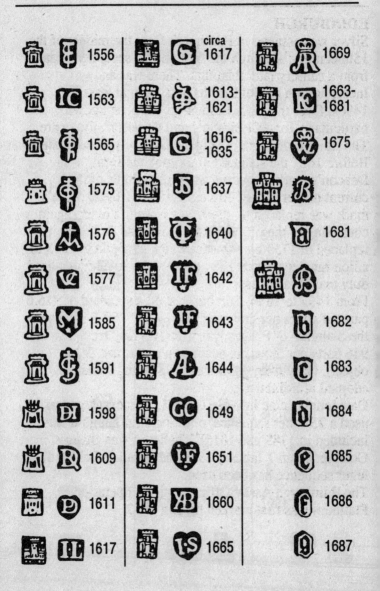

1556	circa 1617	1669
1563	1613-1621	1663-1681
1565	1616-1635	1675
1575	1637	
1576	1640	1681
1577	1642	
1585	1643	1682
1591	1644	1683
1598	1649	1684
1609	1651	1685
1611	1660	1686
1617	1665	1687

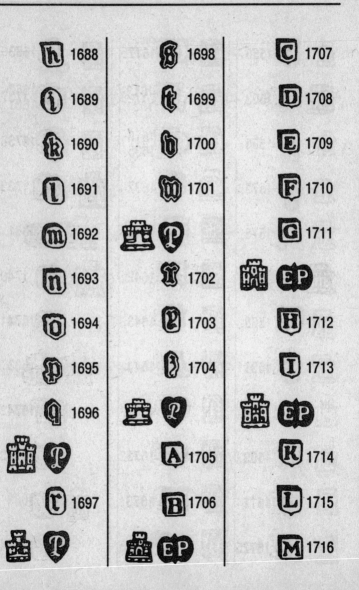

h 1688	s 1698	C 1707
i 1689	t 1699	D 1708
k 1690	b 1700	E 1709
l 1691	w 1701	F 1710
m 1692	P	G 1711
n 1693	r 1702	EP
o 1694	y 1703	H 1712
p 1695	s 1704	I 1713
q 1696	P	EP
P	A 1705	K 1714
r 1697	B 1706	L 1715
P	EP	M 1716

N 1717	V 1725	G 1736
🏰 EP	W 1726	K 1737
O 1718	X 1727	J 1738
P 1719	Y 1728	K 1739
P 1719	Z 1729	🏰 GED
🏰 EP	🏰 AU	L 1740
Q 1720	A 1730	M 1741
R 1721	B 1731	🏰 E·L
S 1722	C 1732	N 1742
T 1723	D 1733	O 1743
U 1724	E 1734	🏰 HG
V 1725	F 1735	P 1744

②	1745	ⓐ	1755	ⓚ	1764
ⓡ	1746	ⓑ	1756	ⓛ	1765
🏰 ⒽⒼ		ⓒ	1757	ⓜ	1766
ⓢ	1747	ⓓ	1758	ⓝ	1767
ⓖ	1748	🏰 Ⓤ		ⓞ	1768
ⓤ	1749	ⓔ	1759	ⓟ	1769
ⓥ	1750	ⓕ	1760	ⓠ	1770
ⓦ	1751	ⓑ	1761	ⓡ	1771
ⓧ	1752	ⓗ	1762		
ⓨ	1753	🏰 Ⓤ			
ⓩ	1754	ⓘ	1763	ⓢ	1772
🏰 ⒽⒼ		ⓘ	1763	ⓡ	1773

These alternative town marks are found circa 1771

🄷 1774		🄵 1785		🄿 1795
🄳 1775		🄶 1786-1787		� 1796
🄸 1776		🄷 1788		
🄳 1777		🄸 1789		🄡 1797
🅉 1778		🄹 1789		🄡 1797
🅄 1779		🄺 1790		🅂 1798
		🄻 1791		
🄰 1780		🄼 1792		🄣 1799
🄱 1781		🄽 1793		🅄 1800
🄲 1782		🄽 1793		🅅 1801
🄳 1783		🄾 1794		
🄴 1784		🄾 1794		🅆 1802

	X	1803				r	1823
	Y	1804		h	1813		
	Z	1805		i	1814		S	1824
				j	1815		t	1825
	a	1806		k	1816			
	b	1807		l	1817		u	1826
	c	1808		m	1818		v	1827
				n	1819		w	1828
	d	1809					X	1829
	e	1810		o	1820		y	1830
	f	1811		p	1821		z	1831
	g	1812		q	1822			

🏷 Ⓐ 1832	🏷 Ⓐ 1844	🏷 Ⓩ 1856
🏷 Ⓑ 1833	🏷 Ⓒ 1845	🏰 🏷
🏷 Ⓒ 1834	🏷 Ⓟ 1846	🏷 Ⓐ 1857
🏷 Ⓓ 1835	🏷 Ⓠ 1847	🏷 Ⓑ 1858
🏷 Ⓔ 1836	🏷 Ⓡ 1848	🏷 Ⓒ 1859
🏷 Ⓕ 1837	🏷 Ⓢ 1849	🏷 Ⓓ 1860
🏷 Ⓖ 1838	🏷 Ⓣ 1850	🏷 Ⓔ 1861
🏷 Ⓗ 1839	🏷 Ⓤ 1851	🏷 Ⓕ 1862
🏷 Ⓘ 1840	🏷 Ⓥ 1852	🏷 Ⓖ 1863
🏷 Ⓚ 1841	🏷 Ⓦ 1853	🏷 Ⓗ 1864
🏷 Ⓛ 1842	🏷 Ⓧ 1854	🏷 Ⓘ 1865
🏷 Ⓜ 1843	🏷 Ⓨ 1855	🏷 Ⓚ 1866

(L)	1867	(X)	1879	(i)	1890
(M)	1868	(Y)	1880	(k)	1891
(N)	1869	(Z)	1881	(l)	1892
(O)	1870			(m)	1893
(P)	1871	(a)	1882	(n)	1894
(Q)	1872	(b)	1883	(o)	1895
(R)	1873	(c)	1884	(p)	1896
(S)	1874	(d)	1885	(q)	1897
(T)	1875	(e)	1886	(r)	1898
(U)	1876	(f)	1887	(s)	1899
(V)	1877	(g)	1888	(t)	1900
(W)	1878	(h)	1889	(v)	1901

Ⓦ 1902	Ⓗ 1913	Ⓤ 1925
Ⓡ 1903	Ⓘ 1914	Ⓥ 1926
Ⓓ 1904	Ⓚ 1915	Ⓦ 1927
Ⓩ 1905	Ⓛ 1916	Ⓧ 1928
	Ⓜ 1917	Ⓨ 1929
Ⓐ 1906	Ⓝ 1918	Ⓩ 1930
Ⓑ 1907	Ⓞ 1919	
Ⓒ 1908	Ⓟ 1920	Ⓐ 1931
Ⓓ 1909	Ⓠ 1921	Ⓑ 1932
Ⓔ 1910	Ⓡ 1922	Ⓒ 1933
Ⓕ 1911	Ⓢ 1923	
Ⓖ 1912	Ⓣ 1924	Ⓓ 1934

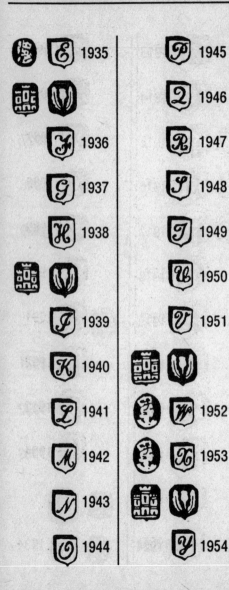

🛡 🛡 1935	🛡 1945	🛡 1955
🏰 🌷	🛡 1946	🏰 🌷
🛡 1936	🛡 1947	🛡 1956
🛡 1937	🛡 1948	🛡 1957
🛡 1938	🛡 1949	🛡 1958
🏰 🌷	🛡 1950	🛡 1959
🛡 1939	🛡 1951	🛡 1960
🛡 1940	🏰 🌷	🛡 1961
🛡 1941	🛡 1952	🛡 1962
🛡 1942	🛡 1953	🛡 1963
🛡 1943	🏰 🌷	🛡 1964
🛡 1944	🛡 1954	🛡 1965

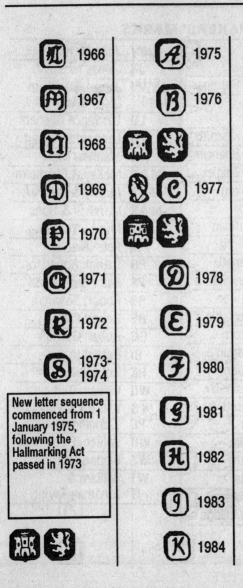

L 1966

M 1967

N 1968

D 1969

P 1970

Q 1971

R 1972

S 1973-1974

New letter sequence commenced from 1 January 1975, following the Hallmarking Act passed in 1973

A 1975

B 1976

C 1977

D 1978

E 1979

F 1980

G 1981

H 1982

I 1983

K 1984

L 1985

M 1986

N 1987

O 1988

P 1989

Q 1990

R 1991

S 1992

T 1993

U 1994

EDINBURGH MAKERS' MARKS

AE	Alexander Edmonstone		JMc	John McKay
			JN	James Nasmyth
AG	Alexander Gairdner		J&WM	James & William Marshall
AH	Alexander Henderson			
			LO	Lawrence Oliphant
AK	Alexander Kincaid		LU	Leonard Urquhart
AS	Alexander Spencer		MC	Matthew Craw
AZ	Alexander Zeigler		M & C	McKay & Chisholm
CD	Charles Dixon		M & F	McKay & Fenwick
E&Co	Elder & Co		M & S	Marshall & Sons
EL	Edward Lothian		MY	Mungo Yorstoun
EO	Edward Oliphant		PM	Peter Mathie
GC	George Christie		PR	Patrick Robertson
GF	George Fenwick		PS	Peter Sutherland
G&K	Gilsland & Ker		RB	Robert Bowman
GMH	George McHattie		RC	Robert Clark
GS	George Scott		RG	Robert Gordon
HB	Henry Beathume		RI	Robert Inglis
HG	Hugh Gordon		RK	Robert Ker
ID	James Dempster		WG	William Ged
IG	John Gilsland		W & PC	William & Peter Cunningham
IK	James Ker			
IR	James Rollo		WR	William Robertson
IW	John Walsh		WS	Walter Scott
IZ	John Zeigler		WT	William & Jonathan Taylor
JD	James Douglas		IT	
JM	Jonathan Millidge			

YORK

The assaying of silver in York dates from the mid 16th century. York silver generally followed Scandinavian styles, and is known for pieces of basic design intended for everyday use. From 1717 to 1776 the York Assay Office was closed, and silver made there was assayed at Newcastle.

The York mark of origin was initially a halved leopard's head conjoined with a halved fleur-de-lys in a round shield. In the late 17th century the halved leopard's head was replaced by a halved seeded rose. This mark underwent numerous changes before, in 1701, it was replaced by a new mark depicting five lions passant on a cross, based on the York City coat of arms. From 1700 to 1850 a leopard's head accompanied the lion passant standard mark on York Sterling silver, while the Britannia mark and lion's head erased were used on York Britannia silver. From 1784 to 1856 (when the York Assay Office closed down), the sovereign's head duty mark was in use.

From at least 1607, York generally used a 24-letter date sequence omitting J and U, then from 1787 a 25-letter sequence omitting just J.

⦿	circa 1568	𝕸	1570	𝕶	1592
⦿	circa 1577	𝕺	1572	𝕷	1593
⦿	circa 1583	𝕻	1573	𝕸	1594
⦿	circa 1594	𝕼	1574	𝕹	1595

Numerous versions of the town mark (see above) were used at the York Assay Office from c1560 to c1606

		𝕽	1575	𝕺	1596
		𝕾	1576	𝕻	1597
		𝕿	1577	𝕼	1598
𝔉	1564	𝖅	1582	𝕽	1599
𝔊	1565	𝖆	1583	𝕿	1601
𝔥	1566	𝖇	1584	𝖗	1604
𝕶	1568	𝖊	1587	⦿	circa 1608
𝕷	1569	𝖍	1590	⦿	circa 1624

From 1607 to 1630, two versions of the town mark (see previous page) were used at the York Assay Office

k 1616

L 1617

M 1618

N 1619

O 1620

P 1621

Q 1622

R 1623

S 1624

T 1625

U 1626

W 1627

X 1628

Y 1629

Z 1630

From 1631 to 1656, two versions of the town mark (see below) were used at York Assay Office

a 1631

b 1632

C 1633

d 1634

e 1635

a 1607

B 1608

C 1609

D 1610

E 1611

F 1612

G 1613

H 1614

J 1615

f	1636	W	1653	H	1664
g	1637	x	1654	J	1665
h	1638	y	1655	K	1666
i	1639	Z	1656	L	1667
k	1641	🌸		M	1668
l	1642	A	1657	N	1669
m	1643	B	1658	Ø	1670
o	1645	C	1659	P	1671
ſ	1649	D	1660	Q	1672
t	1650	E	1661	R	1673
u	1651	F	1662	S	1674
v	1652	G	1663	T	1675

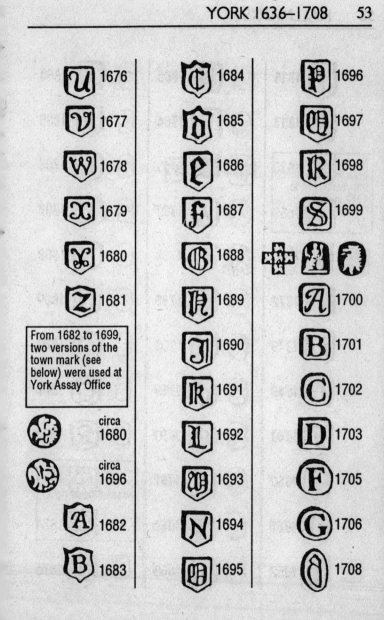

U	1676	C	1684
V	1677	D	1685
W	1678	e	1686
X	1679	F	1687
Y	1680	G	1688
Z	1681	H	1689

From 1682 to 1699, two versions of the town mark (see below) were used at York Assay Office

circa 1680

circa 1696

A	1682	J	1690
B	1683	k	1691
		L	1692
		M	1693
		N	1694
		O	1695

P	1696
Q	1697
R	1698
S	1699
A	1700
B	1701
C	1702
D	1703
F	1705
G	1706
G	1708

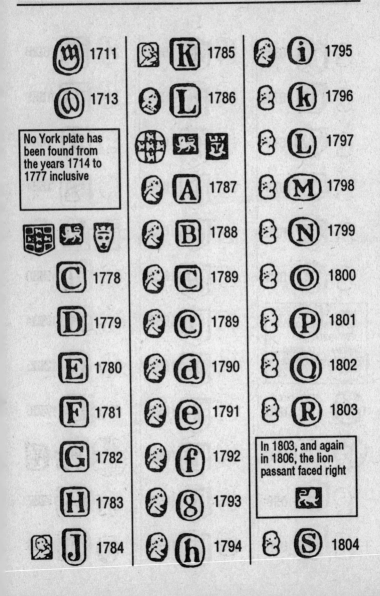

1711

1713

No York plate has been found from the years 1714 to 1777 inclusive

C 1778

D 1779

E 1780

F 1781

G 1782

H 1783

J 1784

K 1785

L 1786

A 1787

B 1788

C 1789

C 1789

d 1790

e 1791

f 1792

g 1793

h 1794

i 1795

k 1796

L 1797

M 1798

N 1799

O 1800

P 1801

Q 1802

R 1803

In 1803, and again in 1806, the lion passant faced right

S 1804

T	1805	e	1816	r	1828
U	1806	F	1817	s	1829
V	1807	g	1818	t	1830
W	1808	h	1819	u	1831
X	1809	i	1820	v	1832
Y	1810	k	1821	w	1833
Z	1811	l	1822	x	1834
		m	1823	y	1835
a	1812	n	1824	z	1836
b	1813	o	1825		
c	1814	p	1826	A	1837
d	1815	q	1827	B	1838

C	1839	
D	1840	P 1851
E	1841	Q 1852
F	1842	R 1853
G	1843	S 1854
H	1844	T 1855
I	1845	V 1856
K	1846	
L	1847	
M	1848	
N	1849	
O	1850	

York Assay Office closed in 1856

YORK MAKERS' MARKS

BC **& N**	James Barber, George Cattle, William North		**JB** **GC** **WN**	James Barber, George Cattle, William North
B & N	James Barber, William North		**JB** **WN**	James Barber, William North
Bu	William Busfield		**JB** **WW**	James Barber, William Whitwell
HP **& C**	John Hampston, John Prince, Robert Cattle		**La**	John Langwith
			Ma	Thomas Mangy
IH **IP**	John Hampston & John Prince		**P** **& Co**	John Prince, Robert Cattle
JB **& Co**	James Barber & Co		**RC** **JB**	Robert Cattle, James Barber

NORWICH

The earliest known Norwich silver marks date from the
mid 16th century. The city is known principally for
ecclesiastical and corporation plate.

The town mark was a lion passant surmounted by a
castle. From the early 17th century another town mark
was also in use, namely a seeded rose crowned, and
variations of both marks appeared until 1701. After
1701, virtually no silver was assayed in Norwich.
Norwich used a 20-letter date sequence (A to V
omitting J). The letter was changed each September.
There are no recorded makers' marks from Norwich.

Town mark	Date letter	Year
	A	1565
	B	1566
	C	1567
	D	1568
	E	1569
	F	1570
	G	1571
	I	1573
	K	1574
	P	1579
		circa 1590
		circa 1595

	circa 1600
	circa 1610
	circa 1620

Several versions of the town marks shown below were used in 1624–1643 (e.g. as above for circa 1620)

Date letter	Year
A	1624
B	1625
C	1626
D	1627
E	1628
F	1629

Date letter	Year
G	1630
H	1631
I	1632
K	1633
L	1634
M	1635
N	1636
O	1637
P	1638
Q	1639
R	1640
S	1641

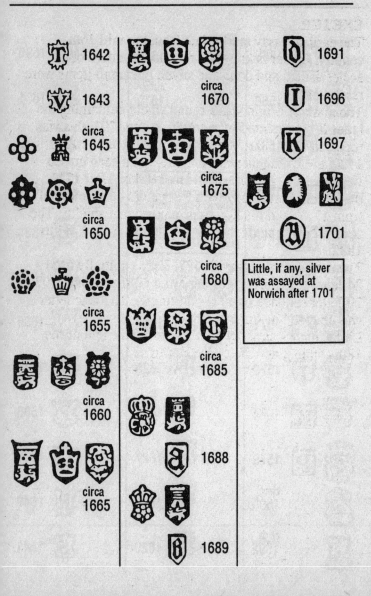

1642

1643

circa 1645

circa 1650

circa 1655

circa 1660

circa 1665

circa 1670

circa 1675

circa 1680

circa 1685

1688

1689

1691

1696

1697

1701

Little, if any, silver was assayed at Norwich after 1701

EXETER

The earliest assay marks date from the mid 16th century. Exeter is known for a good standard of ecclesiastical and domestic silver, but small items were rarely made.

The mark of origin was a round shield containing the letter X surmounted by a crown. After 1701, this was replaced with a three-towered castle. From 1701 to 1720, the Britannia mark and the lion's head erased were in use together as standard marks. After 1721, these were replaced with the leopard's head (omitted from 1777) and the lion passant in square shields. The sovereign's head duty mark was in use from 1784 to 1882.

The date letters began in 1701. Exeter initially used a 24-letter sequence (omitting J and U) then from 1797 a 20-letter sequnce (A to U omitting J). The date letter was changed in August.

Little silver was assayed in Exeter by the end of the 18th century, and the office closed in 1883.

	circa
X IONS	1570
I n	circa 1571
✱ ✱	circa 1575
✱	circa 1580
✱	circa 1585

Various town marks were used at Exeter in about 1630

	circa
♔	1635-1675
✱	1635-1675
✱	circa 1680
✱	circa 1690
✱ 🦁	circa 1690

	circa
♔ X	1698
🏰 🦁 ⚜	
A	1701
B	1702
C	1703
D	1704
E	1705
F	1706
G	1707
H	1708
I	1709
K	1710

L	1711
M	1712
N	1713
O	1714
P	1715
Q	1716
R	1717
S	1718
T	1719
V	1720
🏰 🦁 🦁	
W	1721

X 1722	i 1733	w 1745
Y 1723	k 1734	x 1746
Z 1724	l 1735	y 1747
🛡️ 🛡️ 🛡️	m 1736	z 1748
a 1725	n 1737	🛡️ 🛡️ 🛡️
b 1726	o 1738	A 1749
c 1727	p 1739	B 1750
d 1728	q 1740	C 1751
e 1729	r 1741	D 1752
f 1730	s 1742	E 1753
g 1731	t 1743	F 1754
h 1732	u 1744	G 1755

H	1756	**U**	1768	**F**	1778
I	1757	**W**	1769	**G**	1779
K	1758	**X**	1770	**H**	1780
L	1759	**Y**	1771	**I**	1781–1782
M	1760	**Z**	1772	**K**	1783
N	1761			**L**	1784
O	1762	**A**	1773	**M**	1785
P	1763	**B**	1774	**N**	1786
Q	1764	**C**	1775	**O**	1787
R	1765	**D**	1776	**P**	1788
S	1766	**E**	1777	**q**	1789
T	1767			**r**	1790

🂠 **f** 1791	🂠 **F** 1802	🂠 **R** 1813
🂠 **t** 1792	🂠 **G** 1803	🂠 **S** 1814
🂠 **u** 1793	🂠 **H** 1804	🂠 **T** 1815
🂠 **W** 1794	🏰 🦁	🂠 **U** 1816
🂠 **X** 1795	🂠 **I** 1805	🏰 🦁
🂠 **y** 1796	🂠 **K** 1806	🂠 **a** 1817
🏰 🦁	🂠 **L** 1807	🂠 **b** 1818
🂠 **A** 1797	🂠 **M** 1808	🂠 **c** 1819
🂠 **B** 1798	🂠 **N** 1809	🂠 **d** 1820
🂠 **C** 1799	🂠 **O** 1810	🂠 **e** 1821
🂠 **D** 1800	🂠 **P** 1811	🂠 **f** 1822
🂠 **E** 1801	🂠 **Q** 1812	🂠 **g** 1823

🛡 h 1824	🛡 s 1834	🛡 ℬ 1843
🛡 i 1825	🛡 t 1835	🛡 ℌ 1844
🛡 k 1826	🛡 u 1836	🛡 𝔍 1845
🛡 l 1827	🏛 🦁	🛡 𝔎 1846
🛡 m 1828	🛡 A 1837	🛡 𝔏 1847
🛡 n 1829	🛡 B 1838	🛡 𝔐 1848
🛡 o 1830	🛡 ℭ 1839	🛡 𝔑 1849
🏛 🦁	🛡 𝔇 1840	🛡 𝔒 1850
🛡 p 1831	🏰 🦁	🛡 𝔓 1851
🛡 q 1832	🛡 𝔈 1841	🛡 𝔔 1852
🏛 🦁	🛡 𝔉 1842	🛡 𝔕 1853
🛡 r 1833	🏰 🦁	🛡 𝔖 1854

🙂	𝕿	1855	🙂	**K**	1866	🙂	**A**	1877
🙂	𝖀	1856	🙂	**L**	1867	🙂	**B**	1878
🦁	🦁		🙂	**M**	1868	🙂	**C**	1879
🙂	**A**	1857	🙂	**N**	1869	🙂	**D**	1880
🙂	**B**	1858	🙂	**O**	1870	🙂	**E**	1881
🙂	**C**	1859	🙂	**P**	1871	🙂	**F**	1882
🙂	**D**	1860	🙂	**Q**	1872			
🙂	**E**	1861	🙂	**R**	1873			
🙂	**F**	1862	🙂	**S**	1874			
🙂	**G**	1863	🙂	**T**	1875			
🙂	**H**	1864	🙂	**U**	1876			
🙂	**I**	1865	🦁	🦁				

Exeter Assay Office
closed in 1883

EXETER MAKERS' MARKS

AR	Peter Arno	RF	Richard Ferris
DC	Daniel Coleman	Ri	Edward Richards
El	John Elston	RS	Richard Sams
FR	Richard Freeman	SB	Samuel Blachford
GF	George Ferris	SL	Simon Lery
GT	George Turner	Sy	Pentycost Symonds
IB	John Buck	TB	Thomas Blake
IE	John Elston	TE	Thomas Eustace
IP	Isaac Parkin	TR	George Trowbridge
IW	John Williams	TS	Thomas Sampson
JH	Joseph Hicks	Wi	Richard Wilcocks
JO	John Osmont	WP	William Parry or William Pearse or William Pope
JS	John Stone or James Strong		
JW	James Williams	WRS	W R Sobey
JW & Co	James Whipple & Co	WW	William West
Mo	John Mortimer		

DUBLIN

Dublin's Goldsmiths' Company was given its charter in
1638, although silver had been made there long before
and the Sterling standard was adopted as early as 1606.
Dublin silver is known for a high standard of decorative
workmanship.

The mark of origin is a harp crowned. Originally it also
doubled as the standard mark. Up to 1719, two different
versions of the harp crowned may be found, as shown
in the tables. From 1731 the figure of Hibernia was
added to show that duty had been paid. However, from
1807 when the sovereign's head mark was adopted as a
duty mark (up to 1890, as in England), Hibernia was
kept, and in time became regarded as the mark of origin
for Dublin, while the harp crowned came to be regarded
as the Sterling standard mark.

The date letter sequence began in 1638. Dublin used a
20-letter sequence (A to U omitting J) until 1678, when
a 23 or 24-letter sequence was introduced (omitting J, V
and sometimes I). There was an aborted sequence of A
to C in 1717–19. In 1821 a 25-letter sequence was
adopted (omitting J). The date letter was changed in
June until 1932, since when it has changed in January.
As Dublin is in the Irish Republic, it was not affected
by the United Kingdom's Hallmarking Act of 1973.

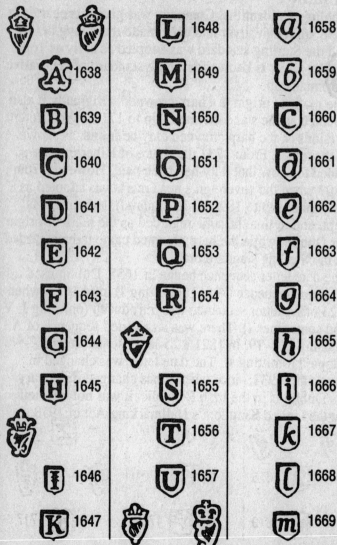

	L 1648	**@** 1658
A 1638	**M** 1649	**b** 1659
B 1639	**N** 1650	**c** 1660
C 1640	**O** 1651	**d** 1661
D 1641	**P** 1652	**e** 1662
E 1642	**Q** 1653	**f** 1663
F 1643	**R** 1654	**g** 1664
G 1644		**h** 1665
H 1645	**S** 1655	**i** 1666
	T 1656	**k** 1667
I 1646	**U** 1657	**l** 1668
K 1647		**m** 1669

🄝 1670	ⓒ 1680	🄳 1703
	🄳 1681	🅁 1704–1705
🄞 1671	ⓔ 1682	🅂 1706–1707
🄟 1672	🄵 1683–1684	ⓣ 1708–1709
🅀 1673	🄶 1685–1687	🅄 1710–1711
🅁 1674	🄷 1688–1693	🅆 1712–1713
🅂 1675	🄺 1694–1695	
🅃 1676	ⓛ 1696–1698	🄴 1714
🅄 1677	🅭 1699	🅈 1715
	🄽 1700	🅉 1716
🄰 1678	🄳 1701	
🄱 1679	🄿 1702	🄰 1717

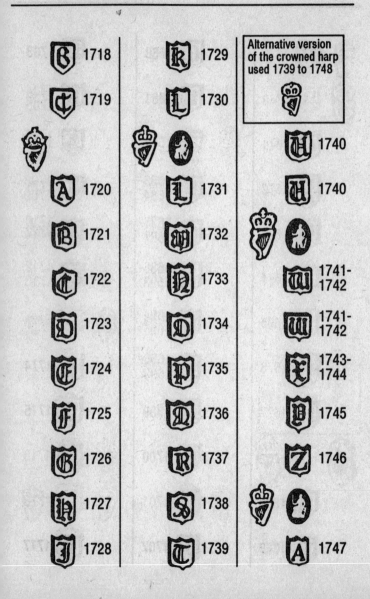

1718	1729	**Alternative version of the crowned harp used 1739 to 1748**
1719	1730	
		1740
1720	1731	1740
1721	1732	1741-1742
1722	1733	1741-1742
1723	1734	1743-1744
1724	1735	1745
1725	1736	1746
1726	1737	
1727	1738	
1728	1739	1747

🛡️ ⚫	🅚 1758	🛡️U 1768
🅱 1748	🅛 1759	🛡️W 1769
🅒 1749	🛡️ ⚫	🛡️X 1770
🅓 1750	🅜 1760	🛡️Y 1771
🅔 1751	🅝 1761	🅩 1772
🅔 1751	🅞 1762	🛡️ ⚫
🅕 1752	🅟 1763	🛡️A 1773
Alternative version of Hibernia used 1751 to 1752 🛡️	🅠 1764	🛡️B 1774
	🅡 1765	🅒 1775
🅖 1753	🅢 1766	🛡️ ⚫
🅗 1754	🛡️ ⚫	🅓 1776
🅤 1757	🅣 1767	🅔 1777

F 1778	**R** 1789	**C** 1799
G 1779	**S** 1790	**D** 1800
H 1780	**T** 1791	**E** 1801
I 1781	**U** 1792	**F** 1802
K 1782	🛡 🦁	**G** 1803
L 1783	**W** 1793	**H** 1804
M 1784	**X** 1794	**I** 1805
N 1785	**Y** 1795	**K** 1806
O 1786	**Z** 1796	👤 **L** 1807
👑 🦁	🛡 🦁	👤 **M** 1808
P 1787	**A** 1797	👤 **N** 1809
Q 1788	**B** 1798	🛡 👑

O	1810	A	1821	I	1829
P	1811	B	1822		
Q	1812	C	1823	K	1830
R	1813	D	1824		
S	1814	E	1825	L	1831
T	1815	e	1825	M	1832
U	1816	F	1826		
W	1817			N	1833
X	1818	G	1827		
Y	1819			O	1834
Z	1820	H	1828	P	1835
				Q	1836

🙂	🛡		🛡	🛡	😊	h 1853
😊	R 1837	😊	Z 1845	😊	h 1853
😊	S 1838	🛡	🛡	😊	j 1854
🛡	🛡	😊	a 1846	🛡	🛡
😊	T 1839	😊	b 1847	😊	k 1855
😊	U 1840	😊	c 1848	😊	l 1856
😊	V 1841	😊	d 1849	😊	m 1857
🛡	🛡	😊	e 1850	😊	n 1858
😊	W 1842	😊	f 1851	😊	O 1859
😊	X 1843	😊	f 1851	😊	P 1860
🛡	🛡	😊	g 1852	😊	Q 1861
😊	Y 1844	😊	g 1852	😊	r 1862

S 1863	C 1873	P 1885
	D 1874	Q 1886
t 1864	E 1875	R 1887
U 1865	F 1876	S 1888
V 1866	G 1877	T 1889
W 1867	H 1878	U 1890
X 1868	I 1879	V 1891
Y 1869	K 1880	W 1892
Z 1870	L 1881	X 1893
	M 1882	Y 1894
A 1871	N 1883	Z 1895
B 1872	O 1884	

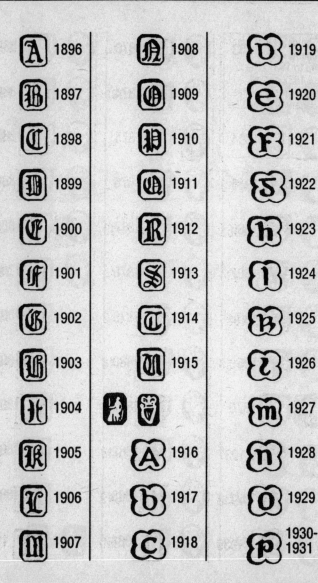

𝕬 1896	𝔑 1908	𝖉 1919
𝕭 1897	𝔒 1909	𝖊 1920
𝕮 1898	𝔓 1910	𝖋 1921
𝕯 1899	𝔔 1911	𝖘 1922
𝕰 1900	𝕽 1912	𝖍 1923
𝕱 1901	𝕾 1913	𝖎 1924
𝕲 1902	𝕿 1914	𝖐 1925
𝕳 1903	𝖀 1915	𝖑 1926
𝕴 1904		𝖒 1927
𝕶 1905	𝕬 1916	𝖓 1928
𝕷 1906	𝖇 1917	𝖔 1929
𝕸 1907	𝖈 1918	𝖕 1930-1931

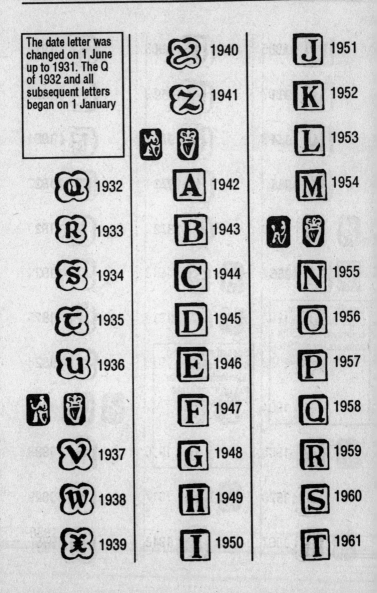

The date letter was changed on 1 June up to 1931. The Q of 1932 and all subsequent letters began on 1 January

1940

1941

1951

1952

1953

1954

1932

1933

1934

1935

1936

A 1942

B 1943

C 1944

D 1945

E 1946

F 1947

G 1948

H 1949

I 1950

1955

1956

P 1957

Q 1958

R 1959

S 1960

T 1961

1937

1938

1939

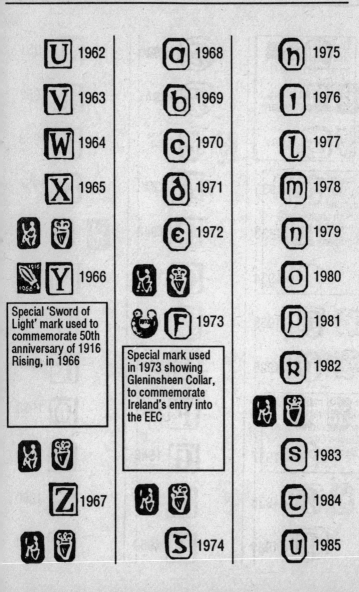

U 1962

V 1963

W 1964

X 1965

Y 1966

Special 'Sword of Light' mark used to commemorate 50th anniversary of 1916 Rising, in 1966

Z 1967

a 1968

b 1969

c 1970

d 1971

e 1972

F 1973

Special mark used in 1973 showing Gleninsheen Collar, to commemorate Ireland's entry into the EEC

s 1974

h 1975

i 1976

l 1977

m 1978

n 1979

o 1980

p 1981

R 1982

S 1983

t 1984

u 1985

[A] 1986

[B] 1987

Special shield used in 1987 to commemorate the 350th anniversary of the Goldsmith's Company of Dublin

[C] 1988

Special mark used in 1988 to commemorate the Dublin City Milennium Year

[D] 1989

[E] 1990

[F] 1991

[G] 1992

[H] 1993

[I] 1994

DUBLIN MAKERS' MARKS

AB	Alexander Brown	JD	James Douglas
AL	Antony Lefebure	JP	John Power
AR	Alexander Richards	J.P	John Pittar
BM	Bartholomew Mosse	JS	James Smythe
CM	Charles Marsh	MH	Michael Hewitson
CT	Christopher Thompson	MN	Michael Nowlan
DE	Daniel Egan	MW	Matthew West
DK	David King	PM	Patrick Moore
EB	Edward Barrett	PW	Peter Walsh
EC	E Crofton	RC	Robert Calderwood
EF	Esther Forbes	RS	Richard Sawyer
EJ	Edmund Johnson	RW	Richard Williams or Robert William
EP	Edward Pome	SN	Samuel Neville
GA	George Alcock	SW	Samuel Walker
GW	George Wheatley	TJ	Thomas Jones
HM	Henry Matthews	TK	Thomas Kinslea
IB	John Buckton	TP	Thomas Parker
IC	John Cuthbert or John Christie	TS	Thomas Slade
IF	John Fry	TW	Thomas Walker
IH	John Hamilton	TWY+	Edward Twycross
II	Joseph Jackson	WA	William Archdall
IL	John Laughlin	WC	William Cummins
ILB	John Le Bas	WL	William Lawson
IP	John Pittar	WN	William Nowlan
IS	James Scott	WR	William Rose
		WW	William Williamson

NEWCASTLE

Silver was assayed in Newcastle from the mid 17th century, becoming systematic in 1702. Newcastle is known for domestic silver, tankards and two-handled cups. A curiosity of Newcastle is the presence of three known women silversmiths.

The town mark depicted three separate castles. From 1702 to 1719, the Britannia mark and the lion's head erased were in use. From 1720, these were replaced with the leopard's head and the lion passant. From 1721 to 1727, the lion passant usually faced to the right. The sovereign's head duty mark was used from 1784 to 1883.

The date letter sequence began in 1702. Newcastle used a 19-letter sequence (A to T generally omitting J) until 1759, when a 24-letter sequence was introduced (omitting J and V). The date letter was changed in May. The Newcastle Assay Office was closed in 1884.

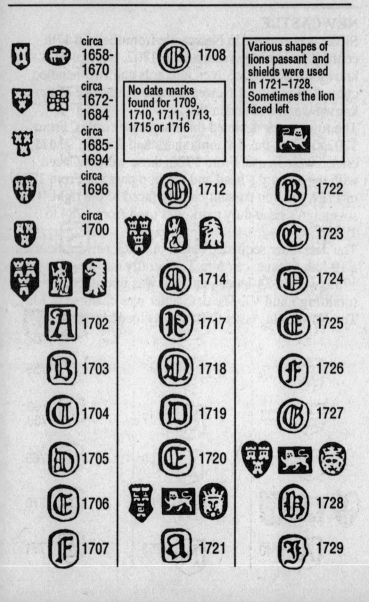

		circa 1658–1670
		circa 1672–1684
		circa 1685–1694
		circa 1696
		circa 1700
	1702	
	1703	
	1704	
	1705	
	1706	
	1707	

	1708

No date marks found for 1709, 1710, 1711, 1713, 1715 or 1716

	1712
	1714
	1717
	1718
	1719
	1720
	1721

Various shapes of lions passant and shields were used in 1721–1728. Sometimes the lion faced left

	1722
	1723
	1724
	1725
	1726
	1727
	1728
	1729

🄺 1730	🄱 1741	🅞 1753
🄻 1731	🄒 1742	🅟 1754
🅦 1732	🄓 1743	🅠 1755
🄝 1733	🄔 1744	🅡 1756
🅦 1734	🄕 1745	🅢 1757
🅟 1735	🄖 1746	🅢 1758
🄞 1736	🄗 1747	🛡 🦁 👑
🄡 1737	🄘 1748	🄰 1759
🄢 1738	🄚 1749	🄱 1760-1768
🄣 1739	🄛 1750	🄲 1769
🛡 🦁 👑	🄜 1751	🄳 1770
🄰 1740	🄝 1752	🄴 1771

🛡 1772	R 1783	D 1794
G 1773	S 1784	E 1795
H 1774	T 1785	F 1796
I 1775	U 1786	G 1797
K 1776	W 1787	H 1798
L 1777	X 1788	I 1799
M 1778	Y 1789	
	Z 1790	K 1800
N 1779		L 1801
O 1780	A 1791	M 1802
P 1781	B 1792	N 1803
Q 1782	C 1793	O 1804

P 1805	B 1816	O 1828
Q 1806	C 1817	P 1829
R 1807	D 1818	Q 1830
S 1808	E 1819	R 1831
T 1809	F 1820	S 1832
U 1810	G 1821	T 1833
W 1811	H 1822	U 1834
X 1812	I 1823	W 1835
Y 1813	K 1824	X 1836
Z 1814	L 1825	Y 1837
	M 1826	Z 1838
A 1815	N 1827	

A 1839
B 1840
C 1841
D 1842
E 1843
F 1844
G 1845
H 1846
I 1847
J 1848
K 1849

L 1850
M 1851
N 1852
O 1853
P 1854
Q 1855
R 1856
S 1857
T 1858
U 1859
W 1860
X 1861

Y 1862
Z 1863
a 1864
b 1865
c 1866
d 1867
e 1868
f 1869
g 1870
h 1871
i 1872

🙂 **k**	1873	Newcastle Assay Office was closed down in 1884
🙂 **l**	1874	
🙂 **m**	1875	
🙂 **n**	1876	
🙂 **o**	1877	
🙂 **p**	1878	
🙂 **q**	1879	
🙂 **r**	1880	
🙂 **s**	1881	
🙂 **t**	1882	
🙂 **u**	1883	

NEWCASTLE MAKERS' MARKS

AK	Alexander Kelty	**IR**	John Robertson
AR	Anne Robertson	**IS**	John Stoddart
Ba	Francis Batty	**IW**	John Walton
Bi	Eli Bilton	**La**	John Langwith
Bu	John Buckle	**L & S**	Lister & Sons
CJR	Christian Reid Junior	**MA**	Mary Ashworth
		Ra	John Ramsay
CR DR	Christian & David Reid	**R & D**	Robertson & Darling
CR IS	Christian Reid & John Stoddart	**RM**	Robert Makepeace
		RP RS	Pinkney & Scott
DC	David Crawford		
DD	David Darling	**RS**	Robert Scott
DL	Dorothy Langlands	**TP**	Thomas Partis
		TS	Thomas Sewill
DR	David Reid	**TW**	Thomas Watson
FB	Francis Batty	**WL**	William Lister
GB	George Bulman	**WL CL WL**	Lister & Sons
IC	Isaac Cookson		
IK	James Kirkup		
IL IR	John Langlands & John Robertson	**Yo**	John Younghusband
IM	John Mitchison		

CHESTER

From the early 15th century, Chester had a guild of goldsmiths which supervised the making, assaying and selling of plate, although marking was not regulated here until the late 17th century. Chester is known for small items such as beakers and creamers.

The mark of origin was the city arms, of a sword between three wheatsheaves (gerbes). From 1701, this changed to three wheatsheaves halved with three lions halved. From 1701 to 1718, the figure of Britannia and the lion's head erased were used as the standard mark. From 1719, the leopard's head crowned and the lion passant were used. From 1839, the leopard's head was omitted. The sovereign's head duty mark was in use from 1784 to 1890.

The date letter sequence began in 1701, and was of irregular length, varying from 21 to 25 letters. The letter was changed each July until 1839, then in August until 1890, then in July again until the office was closed down in 1962.

🛡️🛡️ 1680	I 1709	U 1720
🛡️🛡️ 1690	K 1710	V 1721
STERLING circa 1690–1700	L 1711	W 1722
🛡️🛡️🛡️	M 1712	X 1723
A 1701	N 1713	Y 1724
B 1702	O 1714	Z 1725
C 1703	P 1715	🛡️🛡️🛡️
D 1704	Q 1716	A 1726
E 1705	R 1717	B 1727
F 1706	S 1718	C 1728
G 1707	🛡️🛡️🛡️	D 1729
H 1708	T 1719	E 1730

F 1731	*S* 1743	C 1753
G 1732	*T* 1744	d 1754
K 1733	*U* 1745	e 1755
J 1734	*V* 1746	f 1756
K 1735	*W* 1747	G 1757
L 1736	X 1748	h 1758
M 1737	Y 1749	i 1759
N 1738	*Y* 1749	k 1760
O 1739	*Z* 1750	l 1761
P 1740		m 1762
Q 1741	a 1751	n 1763
R 1742	b 1752	O 1764

P 1765	a 1776	l 1786
Q 1766	b 1777	m 1787
R 1767	c 1778	n 1788
S 1768	(shield) (lion) (head)	o 1789
T 1769	d 1779	p 1790
T 1770	e 1780	q 1791
U 1771	f 1781	r 1792
V 1772	g 1782	s 1793
W 1773	h 1783	t 1794
X 1774	(head) (lion) (crown)	u 1795
Y 1775	(head) i 1784	v 1796
(shield) (lion) (head)	(head) k 1785	(shield) (lion) (head)

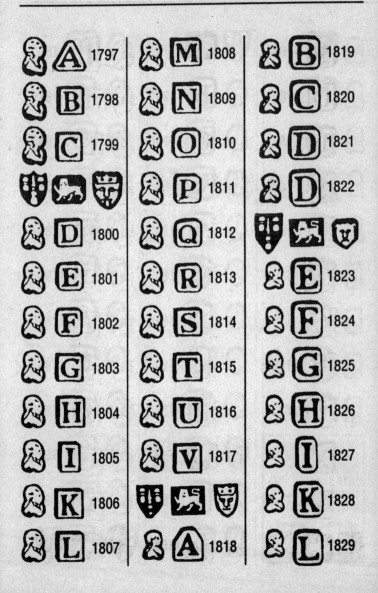

A 1797	M 1808	B 1819
B 1798	N 1809	C 1820
C 1799	O 1810	D 1821
(shields)	P 1811	D 1822
D 1800	Q 1812	(shields)
E 1801	R 1813	E 1823
F 1802	S 1814	F 1824
G 1803	T 1815	G 1825
H 1804	U 1816	H 1826
I 1805	V 1817	I 1827
K 1806	(shields)	K 1828
L 1807	A 1818	L 1829

🙂	**M**	1830	🛡️	🦁		🙂	**M**	1850
🙂	**N**	1831	🙂	**A**	1839	🙂	**N**	1851
🙂	**O**	1832	🙂	**B**	1840	🙂	**O**	1852
🙂	**P**	1833	🙂	**C**	1841	🙂	**P**	1853
🙂	**Q**	1834	🙂	**D**	1842	🙂	**Q**	1854
🙂	**R**	1835	🙂	**E**	1843	🙂	**R**	1855
🙂	**S**	1836	🙂	**F**	1844	🙂	**S**	1856
🙂	**T**	1837	🙂	**G**	1845	🙂	**T**	1857
🙂	**U**	1838	🙂	**H**	1846	🙂	**U**	1858

Two shield shapes are found for the Sterling mark from 1839 onwards, and also for the date letter from 1900

🙂	**I**	1847	🙂	**B**	1859
🙂	**K**	1848	🙂	**W**	1860
🙂	**L**	1849	🙂	**X**	1861

	1862		k	1873			
	1863		l	1874		A	1884
	a	1864		m	1875		B	1885
	b	1865		n	1876		C	1886
	c	1866		o	1877		D	1887
	d	1867		p	1878		E	1888
	e	1868		q	1879		F	1889
	f	1869		r	1880			
	g	1870		s	1881		G	1890
	h	1871		t	1882		H	1891
	i	1872		u	1883		I	1892
							K	1893

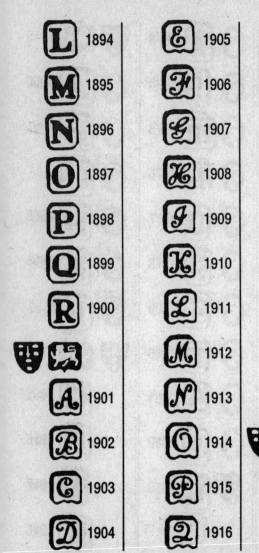

L 1894	**E** 1905	**R** 1917
M 1895	**F** 1906	**S** 1918
N 1896	**G** 1907	**T** 1919
O 1897	**H** 1908	**U** 1920
P 1898	**I** 1909	**V** 1921
Q 1899	**K** 1910	**W** 1922
R 1900	**L** 1911	**X** 1923
	M 1912	**Y** 1924
A 1901	**N** 1913	**Z** 1925
B 1902	**O** 1914	
C 1903	**P** 1915	**a** 1926
D 1904	**Q** 1916	**B** 1927

T 1928	**A** 1938	**Y** 1949
D 1929	**Q** 1939	**Z** 1950
e 1930	**P** 1940	**A** 1951
ff 1931	**Q** 1941	🛡 🦁
G 1932	**R** 1942	👤 **B** 1952
H 1933	**S** 1943	👤 **C** 1953
🛡 🦁	**Z** 1944	🛡 🦁
👁 **J** 1934	**U** 1945	**D** 1954
👁 **K** 1935	**V** 1946	**E** 1955
🛡 🦁	**W** 1947	**F** 1956
L 1936	🛡 🦁	**G** 1957
M 1937	**X** 1948	**H** 1958

J 1959	**L** 1961	Chester Assay Office closed in August 1962
K 1960	**M** 1962	

CHESTER MAKERS' MARKS

B & F	Matthew Boulton & James Fothergill	**JA**	John Adamson
Bi	Charles Bird	**JC**	James Conway or John Coakley
BP	Benjamin Pemberton	**JL**	John Lowe
Bu	Nathaniel Bullen	**JS**	John Sutters
Du	Bartholomew Duke	**NC**	Nicholas Cunliffe
EM	Edward Maddock	**Pe**	Peter Pemberton
FB	Francis Butt	**RG**	Robert Green
GL	George Lowe	**RI**	Robert Jones
GR	George Roberts	**RL**	Robert Lowe
GW	George Walker	**RP**	Richard Pike
IB	James Barton	**RR**	Richard Richardson
IG	John Gilbert	**TM**	Thomas Maddock
IL TL	John & Thomas Lowe	**WH**	William Hull
IR	John Richards	**WP**	William Pugh
IW	Joseph Walley	**WR**	William Richardson

GLASGOW

Silver was assayed in Glasgow from the late 17th century, although in the years 1784–1819 Glasgow silverware was mainly assayed in Edinburgh. In the latter year the Glasgow Goldsmiths' Company was formed and several changes were made in the marks. The Glasgow mark of origin was a tree with a bird in the upper branches, a bell hanging from a lower branch and a fish (with a ring in its mouth) laid across the trunk. From 1819, a lion rampant was adopted as the Sterling standard mark, and in 1914 the Scottish thistle was added. Also from 1819, the Britannia standard (and appropriate mark) were in optional use. Up to 1784, the maker's mark was stamped twice, once on each side of the mark of origin. The sovereign's head duty mark was used from 1819 to 1890.

The date letter sequence began in 1681. After about the first 25 years, regular cycles were abandoned and the letters 's' and 'o' were commonly used until 1819, when a full 26-letter sequence was introduced. The date letter was changed annually in July.

The Glasgow Assay Office closed in 1964.

Date letters were used in 1681-1709, but then not again until 1819

The maker's mark was stamped on both sides of the Glasgow town mark up to 1784

 a 1681

 C 1683

 e 1685

 i 1689

 K 1690

 O 1694

O 1696

S 1698

t 1699

II 1700

U 1701

P 1704

Y 1705

B circa 1707

D circa 1709

circa 1717

The letter S was used probably as a Sterling mark

S circa 1728

S circa 1734

S circa 1743

S circa 1747

S circa 1756

circa 1757

S circa 1758

E circa 1763

S circa 1773

S circa 1773

O circa 1776

S circa 1780

S circa 1781

S circa 1783

		circa						
	S	1784		I	1827		T	1838
		1811		J	1828		U	1839
				K	1829		V	1840
	A	1819		L	1830		W	1841
				M	1831		X	1842
	B	1820		N	1832		Y	1843
	C	1821		O	1833		Z	1844
	D	1822		P	1834			
	E	1823		Q	1835		A	1845
	F	1824		R	1836		B	1846
	G	1825					C	1847
	H	1826		S	1837		D	1848

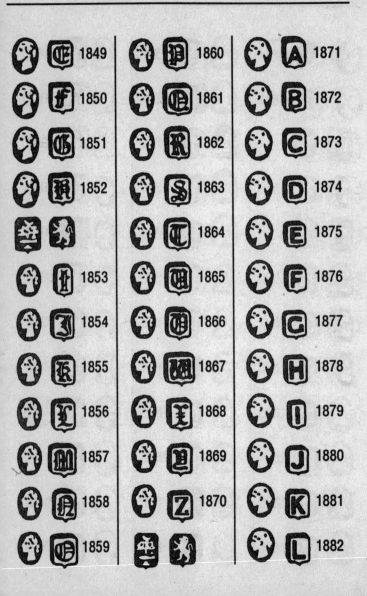

1849	1860	1871
1850	1861	1872
1851	1862	1873
1852	1863	1874
	1864	1875
1853	1865	1876
1854	1866	1877
1855	1867	1878
1856	1868	1879
1857	1869	1880
1858	1870	1881
1859		1882

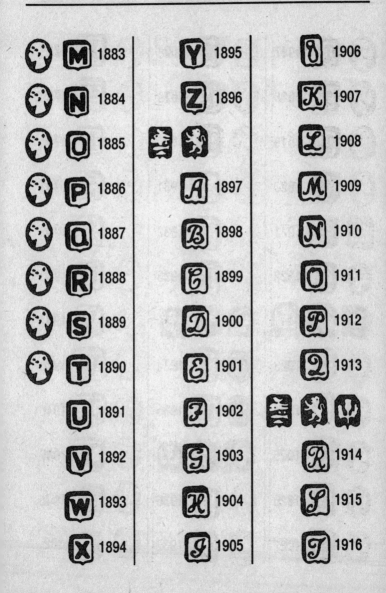

M 1883	Y 1895	8 1906
N 1884	Z 1896	K 1907
O 1885	1897	L 1908
P 1886	A 1897	M 1909
Q 1887	B 1898	N 1910
R 1888	C 1899	O 1911
S 1889	D 1900	P 1912
T 1890	E 1901	Q 1913
U 1891	F 1902	R 1914
V 1892	G 1903	S 1915
W 1893	H 1904	T 1916
X 1894	J 1905	

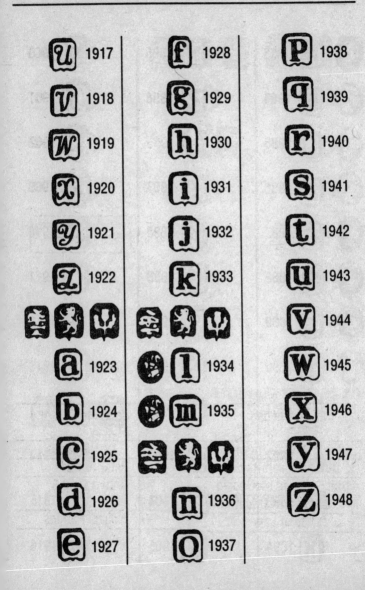

𝒰 1917	f 1928	P 1938
𝒱 1918	g 1929	q 1939
𝒲 1919	h 1930	r 1940
𝒳 1920	i 1931	s 1941
𝒴 1921	j 1932	t 1942
𝒵 1922	k 1933	u 1943
a 1923	l 1934	v 1944
b 1924	m 1935	w 1945
c 1925		x 1946
d 1926	n 1936	y 1947
e 1927	o 1937	z 1948

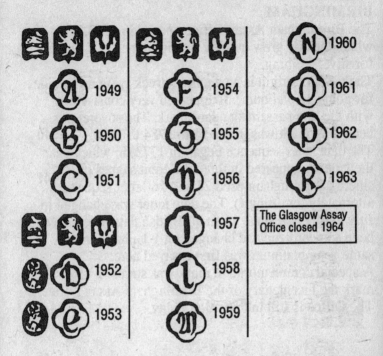

	1960
1949	1954	1961
1950	1955	1962
1951	1956	1963
	1957	
1952	1958	
1953	1959	

The Glasgow Assay Office closed 1964

GLASGOW MAKERS' MARKS

AM	Alexander Mitchell	**JM**	John Mitchell or J Murray
A & T	Aird & Thompson	**LFN**	Luke Newlands
DCR	Duncan Rait	**PA**	Peter Arthur
DMcD	David McDonald	**RG & S**	Robert Gray & Sons
JC	James Crichton	**WP**	William Parkins
JL	John Law		

BIRMINGHAM

The Birmingham Assay Office opened in 1773, after which the city grew quickly in importance as a centre for silversmithing.

The mark of origin is an anchor (struck lying on its side for gold and platinum). It appeared very consistently with the lion passant standard mark. The sovereign's head duty mark was in use from 1784 to 1890.

The date letter sequence began in 1773 (in which year the letter A appeared in three different shapes of shield). Birmingham used 25 and 26-letter sequences alternately (omitting J). The date letter was changed in July until 1975, since when all British date letters have been standardized and changed on 1 January. In the same year, platinum was first assayed here.

A special commemorative mark was struck in 1973 to mark the bicentenary of the Birmingham Assay Office. The Office is still in operation today.

🔗 🦁	K 1782	👤 W 1794
A 1773	L 1783	👤 X 1795
A 1773	M 1784	👤 Y 1796
A 1773	N 1785	👤 Z 1797
B 1774	O 1786	
C 1775	P 1787	
D 1776	Q 1788	
E 1777	R 1789	
F 1778	S 1790	🔗 🦁
G 1779	T 1791	👤 a 1798
H 1780	U 1792	👤 b 1799
I 1781	V 1793	👤 c 1800
		👤 d 1801

The duty on silver was doubled in 1797, and so for a short time the King's head was stamped twice

e	1802	q	1814	B	1825
f	1803	r	1815	C	1826
g	1804	s	1816	D	1827
h	1805	t	1817	E	1828
i	1806	u	1818	F	1829
j	1807	v	1819	G	1830
k	1808	w	1820	H	1831
l	1809	x	1821	J	1832
m	1810	y	1822	K	1833
n	1811	z	1823	L	1834
o	1812			M	1835
p	1813	A	1824	N	1836

🜨	𝕯	1837	⚓	🦁		🜨	𝕷	1860
🜨	𝕻	1838	🜨	**A**	1849	🜨	**M**	1861
🜨	𝕺	1839	🜨	**B**	1850	🜨	**N**	1862
🜨	𝕽	1840	🜨	**C**	1851	🜨	**O**	1863
🜨	𝕾	1841	🜨	**D**	1852	🜨	**P**	1864
🜨	𝕿	1842	🜨	**E**	1853	🜨	**Q**	1865
🜨	𝖀	1843	🜨	**F**	1854	🜨	**R**	1866
🜨	𝖁	1844	🜨	**G**	1855	⚓	🦁	
🜨	𝖂	1845	🜨	**H**	1856	🜨	**S**	1867
🜨	𝖃	1846	🜨	**I**	1857	🜨	**T**	1868
🜨	𝖄	1847	🜨	**J**	1858	🜨	**U**	1869
🜨	**Z**	1848	🜨	**K**	1859	🜨	**V**	1870

🙂 Ⓦ 1871	🙂 ⓗ 1882	ⓡ 1891
🙂 Ⓧ 1872	⚓ 🦁	ⓢ 1892
🙂 Ⓨ 1873	🙂 ⓘ 1883	ⓣ 1893
🙂 Ⓩ 1874	🙂 ⓚ 1884	ⓤ 1894
⚓ 🦁	🙂 ⓛ 1885	ⓥ 1895
🙂 ⓐ 1875	🙂 ⓜ 1886	ⓜ 1896
🙂 ⓑ 1876	🙂 ⓝ 1887	ⓧ 1897
🙂 ⓒ 1877	🙂 ⓞ 1888	ⓨ 1898
🙂 ⓓ 1878	🙂 ⓟ 1889	ⓩ 1899
🙂 ⓔ 1879	🙂 ⓠ 1890	⚓ 🦁
🙂 ⓕ 1880	The Queen's head duty mark was not used after 1890	ⓐ 1900
🙂 ⓖ 1881		ⓑ 1901

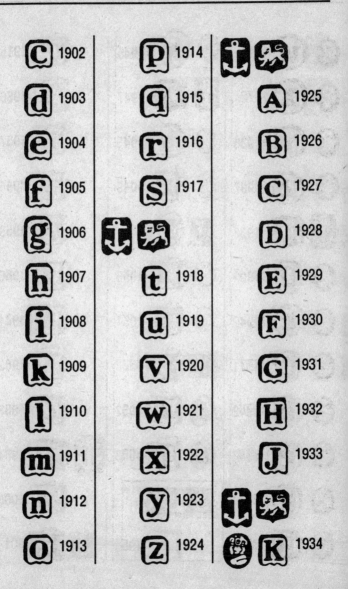

ⓒ 1902	℗ 1914	(anchor)(lion)
ⓓ 1903	ⓠ 1915	Ⓐ 1925
ⓔ 1904	ⓡ 1916	Ⓑ 1926
ⓕ 1905	Ⓢ 1917	Ⓒ 1927
ⓖ 1906	(anchor)(lion)	Ⓓ 1928
ⓗ 1907	ⓣ 1918	Ⓔ 1929
ⓘ 1908	ⓤ 1919	Ⓕ 1930
ⓚ 1909	Ⓥ 1920	Ⓖ 1931
ⓛ 1910	Ⓦ 1921	Ⓗ 1932
ⓜ 1911	Ⓧ 1922	Ⓙ 1933
ⓝ 1912	ⓨ 1923	(anchor)(lion)
Ⓞ 1913	Ⓩ 1924	(crown)Ⓚ 1934

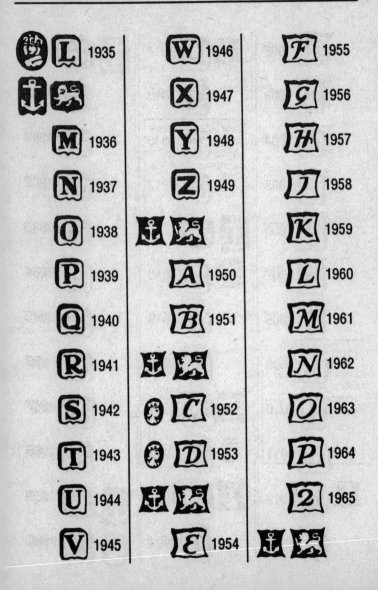

🦁 L 1935	W 1946	F 1955
⚓ 🦁	X 1947	C 1956
M 1936	Y 1948	H 1957
N 1937	Z 1949	J 1958
O 1938	⚓ 🦁	K 1959
P 1939	A 1950	L 1960
Q 1940	B 1951	M 1961
R 1941	⚓ 🦁	N 1962
S 1942	👑 C 1952	O 1963
T 1943	👑 D 1953	P 1964
U 1944	⚓ 🦁	2 1965
V 1945	E 1954	⚓ 🦁

R 1966

S 1967

T 1968

U 1969

V 1970

W 1971

X 1972

In 1973 the bicentenary of the Birmingham Assay Office was commemorated by a special town mark

Y 1973

Z 1974

New letter sequence commenced from 1 January 1975, in accordance with the Hallmarking Act passed in 1973

A 1975

B 1976

C 1977

D 1978

E 1979

F 1980

G 1981

H 1982

I 1983

K 1984

L 1985

M 1986

N 1987

O 1988

P 1989

Q 1990

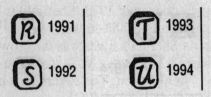

Ⓡ	1991	Ⓣ	1993
Ⓢ	1992	Ⓤ	1994

BIRMINGHAM MAKERS' MARKS

C & B	Cocks & Bettridge	MB	Matthew Boulton
E & CoLd	Elkington & Co	MB IF	Matthew Boulton & John Fothergill
EM & Co	Elkington Mason & Co	ML	Matthew Linwood
ES	Edward Smith	NM	Nathaniel Mills
ET	Edward Thomasson	P & T	William Postan & George Tye
FC	Francis Clark		
GU	George Unite	REA	Robinson, Edkins & Aston
GW	Gervase Wheeler		
H & T	Hilliard & Thomasson	SP	Samuel Pemberton
		T & P	Joseph Taylor & John Perry
IB	John Bettridge		
IS	John Shaw	TS	Thomas Shaw
IT	Joseph Taylor	TW	Thomas Willmore
JW	Joseph Willmore	WF	William Fowke
L & Co	John Lawrence & Co	Y & W	Yapp & Woodward

SHEFFIELD

The Assay Office was opened in 1773. Sheffield is best known for the production of candlesticks.

The mark of origin on Sheffield silver was the crown until 1975, since when it has been a York rose. The standard mark was a lion passant. The sovereign's head duty mark was in use from 1784 to 1890.

From 1780 to 1853, small items were marked with a special stamp on which the crown mark of origin and the date letter were combined.

The application of date letters began in September 1773 with the letter E, changing every July. The choice of letter was quite random until 1824, when Sheffield began to use a regular 25-letter alphabetical sequence (omitting J). In 1975, the standard British date letter sequence was imposed, with the letter being changed on 1 January each year. In the same year, platinum was first assayed at Sheffield.

The Sheffield Assay Office is still in operation.

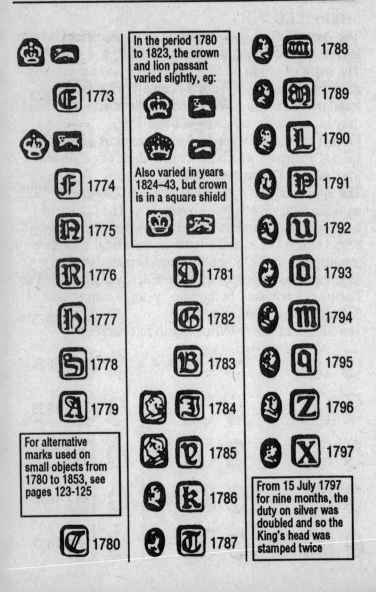

1773

1774

1775

1776

1777

1778

1779

For alternative marks used on small objects from 1780 to 1853, see pages 123-125

1780

In the period 1780 to 1823, the crown and lion passant varied slightly, eg:

Also varied in years 1824–43, but crown is in a square shield

1781

1782

1783

1784

1785

1786

1787

1788

1789

1790

1791

1792

1793

1794

1795

1796

1797

From 15 July 1797 for nine months, the duty on silver was doubled and so the King's head was stamped twice

V 1798	L 1810	Z 1822
E 1799	C 1811	U 1823
N 1800	D 1812	a 1824
H 1801	R 1813	b 1825
M 1802	W 1814	c 1826
F 1803	O 1815	d 1827
G 1804	T 1816	e 1828
B 1805	X 1817	f 1829
A 1806	I 1818	g 1830
S 1807	V 1819	h 1831
P 1808	Q 1820	k 1832
K 1809	Y 1821	l 1833

🙂 **m** 1834	🙂 **B** 1845	🙂 **O** 1857
🙂 **P** 1835	🙂 **C** 1846	🙂 **P** 1858
🙂 **q** 1836	🙂 **D** 1847	🙂 **R** 1859
🙂 **r** 1837	🙂 **E** 1848	🙂 **S** 1860
🙂 **S** 1838	🙂 **F** 1849	🙂 **T** 1861
🙂 **t** 1839	🙂 **G** 1850	🙂 **U** 1862
🙂 **u** 1840	🙂 **H** 1851	🙂 **V** 1863
🙂 **V** 1841	🙂 **I** 1852	🙂 **W** 1864
🙂 **X** 1842	🙂 **K** 1853	🙂 **X** 1865
🙂 **Z** 1843	🙂 **L** 1854	🙂 **Y** 1866
😀 🦁	🙂 **M** 1855	🙂 **Z** 1867
🙂 **A** 1844	🙂 **N** 1856	👑 🦁

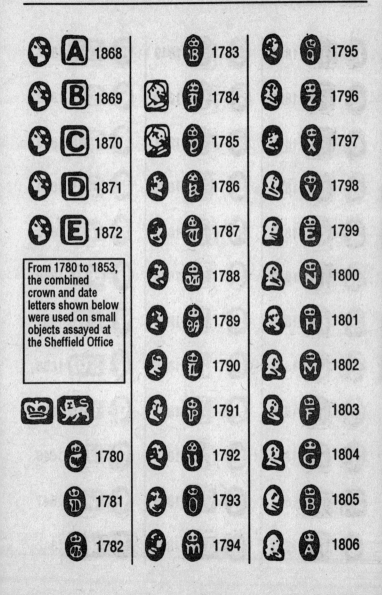

		1868
		1869
		1870
		1871
		1872

From 1780 to 1853, the combined crown and date letters shown below were used on small objects assayed at the Sheffield Office

	1780
	1781
	1782

	1783
	1784
	1785
	1786
	1787
	1788
	1789
	1790
	1791
	1792
	1793
	1794

	1795
	1796
	1797
	1798
	1799
	1800
	1801
	1802
	1803
	1804
	1805
	1806

S	1807	
P	1808	
K	1809	
L	1810	
C	1811	
D	1812	
R	1813	
W	1814	
O	1815	
T	1816	
X	1817	
I	1818	

V	1819	
Q	1820	
Y	1821	
Z	1822	
U	1823	
a	1824	
b	1825	
c	1826	
d	1827	
e	1828	
f	1829	
g	1830	

h	1831	
k	1832	
l	1833	
E	1834	
P	1835	
q	1836	
r	1837	
s	1838	
t	1839	
u	1840	
v	1841	
x	1842	

Z 1843	F 1873	S 1885
A 1844	G 1874	T 1886
B 1845	H 1875	U 1887
C 1846	J 1876	V 1888
D 1847	K 1877	W 1889
E 1848	L 1878	X 1890
F 1849	M 1879	Y 1891
G 1850	N 1880	Z 1892
H 1851	O 1881	
I 1852	P 1882	a 1893
K 1853	Q 1883	b 1894
	R 1884	c 1895

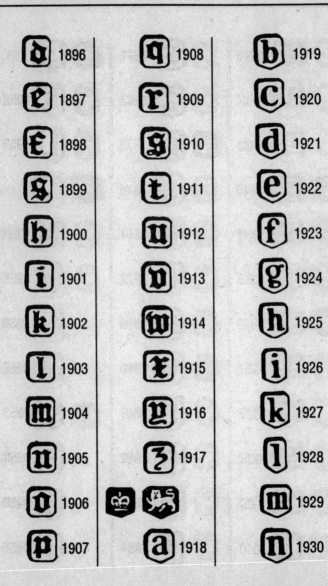

d 1896

e 1897

f 1898

g 1899

h 1900

i 1901

k 1902

l 1903

m 1904

n 1905

o 1906

p 1907

q 1908

r 1909

s 1910

t 1911

u 1912

v 1913

w 1914

x 1915

y 1916

z 1917

a 1918

b 1919

c 1920

d 1921

e 1922

f 1923

g 1924

h 1925

i 1926

k 1927

l 1928

m 1929

n 1930

1931	O
1932	P
1933	q
1934	r
1935	s
1936	t
1937	u
1938	V
1939	W
1940	X
1941	y
1942	Z
1943	A
1944	B
1945	C
1946	D
1947	E
1948	F
1949	G
1950	H
1951	I
1952	K
1953	L
1954	M
1955	N
1956	O
1957	P
1958	Q
1959	R
1960	S
1961	T

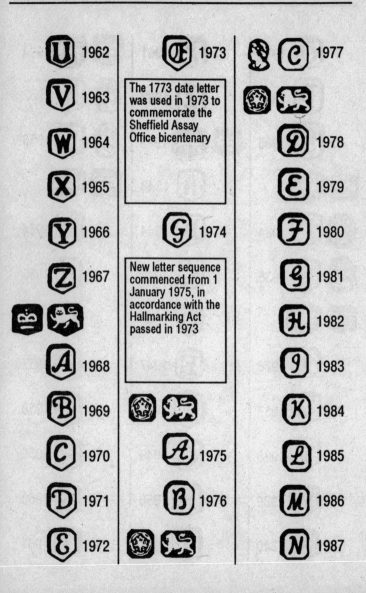

U 1962

V 1963

W 1964

X 1965

Y 1966

Z 1967

A 1968

B 1969

C 1970

D 1971

E 1972

F 1973

The 1773 date letter was used in 1973 to commemorate the Sheffield Assay Office bicentenary

G 1974

New letter sequence commenced from 1 January 1975, in accordance with the Hallmarking Act passed in 1973

A 1975

B 1976

C 1977

D 1978

E 1979

F 1980

G 1981

H 1982

I 1983

K 1984

L 1985

M 1986

N 1987

Ⓞ 1988	Ⓡ 1991	Ⓤ 1994
Ⓟ 1989	Ⓢ 1992	
Ⓠ 1990	Ⓣ 1993	

SHEFFIELD MAKERS' MARKS

AH	Aaron Hadfield	**JC** **NC**	J & N Creswick
DH & Co	Daniel Holy & Co		
D & S	Dixon & Sons	**JD & S**	James Dixon & Sons
GA **& Co**	George Ashforth & Co		
		JR	J Round & Son
GE **& Co**	George Eadon & Co	**MF** **RC**	Fenton, Creswick & Co
HA	Henry Archer & Co	**MH** **& Co**	Martin Hall & Co
H & H	Howard & Hawksworth	**NS & Co**	Nathaniel Smith & Co
HE **& Co**	Hawksworth, Eyre & Co	**RM**	Richard Morton
HT	Henry Tudor	**RM** **& Co**	Richard Morton & Co
HW **& Co**	Henry Wilkinson & Co	**RM** **EH**	Remy Martin & Edward Hall
IG & Co	John Green & Co	**S & N**	Stafford & Newton
IH **& Co**	J Hoyland & Co	**SR & Co**	Samuel Roberts & Co
IL	John Law	**T & IS**	T & I Settle
IP & Co	John Parsons & Co	**TJ** **NC**	TJ & N Creswick
IR & Co	John Roberts & Co		
ITY **& Co**	John T Younge & Co	**WD**	William Damant
IW **& Co**	John Winter & Co	**WF** **AF**	Fordham & Faulkner
JB	James Burbury	**W & H**	Walker & Hall